Marked By Prayer

A PARENTS' PRAYER JOURNAL FOR THE
2020–2021 SCHOOL YEAR

CYNTHIA YANOF

PARDON
The Mess

christian parenting

PERFECTLY, IMPERFECT.

Marked By Prayer

"THAT'S GONNA LEAVE A MARK."

Those five words pretty well sum up my childhood growing up with twin brothers who were five years older than me. I can appreciate a little sibling rivalry with the best of them, but my older brothers were relentless back in the day.

Let's see. There was the time I was riding my shiny new bike full speed down our street when one of them threw a broomstick through the spokes. Or the time when my parents left them to babysit and they put me in the closet with a mattress covering me in case a tornado hit (in a town that, to this day, has never experienced a tornado). I won't even go there with the training bra incident in fifth grade… I have no words.

Thankfully, we grew up to love each other, and I even "appreciate" some of their childhood antics now.

As parents, we're navigating the uncharted territory of raising kids in a culture inundated with technology, gender-identity issues, school shootings, social media, a pandemic, and more. With all of the things threatening to mark our kids' childhood, God wants to mark them with a faith that transforms their lives from the inside out.

The fact is, we have no idea what God will call our kids to do someday. The Bible is packed with stories of ordinary people called to do seemingly impossible things. What made them stand out for God's purposes? They were marked by a faith God could use for significance and impact far beyond what they (or their parents) could have ever imagined.

Consider this.

- Noah didn't know he would face forty days and forty nights in a flood, but he was *marked by obedience* to build an ark having never seen rain.
- Daniel didn't know he would end up in a lions' den, but he was *marked by conviction* to never compromise his beliefs.
- Moses didn't know he would be called to lead an entire people out of slavery, but he was *marked by faith* in God's greater plans despite his inadequacies.
- Mary didn't know she would give birth to the Messiah, but she was *marked by God's calling* no matter the personal cost.

What can we do to raise up the next generation of Noah, Daniel, Moses, and Mary—those marked by obedience, conviction, faith, and God's calling?

It's not easy, for sure. But a great starting place is on our knees. When we're marked by prayer as parents, it leaves a mark on our kids (and not the kind my brothers left on me).

Beginning a new school year is the perfect time to renew our commitment to praying for our children. Let's challenge ourselves to pray more than just safety and well-being over them, but to pray that their lives are marked by the only One who shapes lives and transforms people into kingdom-building vessels.

In this with you,

Cynthia Yanof

CYNTHIA YANOF
PARDON THE MESS

We're thrilled that you're joining our prayer journey this school year.

Each of the following pages provides a topic we're praying, as well as related Scripture to use as a reference point. We're praying each week that our kids are marked by things like faith, an undivided heart, hope, direction, and compassion.

You will also notice that there are opportunities to journal each week, noting the areas where you're grateful as well as the requests you're bringing to the Lord on behalf of your family. Our hope is that you will take time to make specific notes on what you're praying and even share that with your kids.

What a testament to God's faithfulness if, at the end of the year, we can look back and point to the places where we prayed over our kids and God answered with a resounding yes.

Our hope is that this little book guides and encourages you as you pray for your kids. Keep it in the car, on the bathroom counter, in the kitchen, or anywhere that will remind you to come before the Lord on behalf of your family.

And if you have not already, take a minute to utilize our "texting truth" program that sends personalized Scripture to your t(w)een's cell phone each day. The verses they receive each day will correspond with the week's theme in this book. In other words, if you're praying faith for your child one week, they will receive personalized Scripture each day speaking to faith.

To sign up, simply text the words **"textingtruth"** to **55588** from the phone where you want to receive daily verses.

Marked By Wisdom

"AND JESUS GREW IN WISDOM AND STATURE, AND IN FAVOR WITH GOD AND MAN."

LUKE 2:52

The Bible gives us little glimpses of Jesus as he was growing up, like the reference in Luke that he grew in wisdom, stature, and favor. As we kick off a new school year, it seems appropriate to pray for the same areas of growth for our family that Jesus experienced.

The world values the wisdom found in history, art, literature, and music, but, as believers, we're reminded that *true* wisdom comes only from God (Matthew 6:33).

Solomon was given the opportunity to ask God for anything when he became king. Feeling inadequate to fill David's shoes, he asked for wisdom to govern his people well. God was so pleased with his request that he gave Solomon greater wisdom than any other man (along with lots of wealth). What a great reminder that God's wisdom is unparalleled and that he's generous to give it to those who ask.

As we pray for kids marked by wisdom, let's pray that they are receptive to God's instruction and resolved to live in the wisdom it provides. The world has lots of wisdom counterfeits; pray that our kids seek the only true source, Jesus.

JAMES 1:5   COLOSSIANS 4:5–6   PROVERBS 2:6   JAMES 3:17

I'm grateful for:

_____

_____

_____

_____

_____

_____

_____

I'm praying for:

_____

_____

_____

_____

_____

_____

_____

prayer:

Lord, your wisdom is more precious than gold and you generously offer it to all who ask. Provide [name] with wisdom in the words they speak and the roads they walk. Give my family a desire to always seek your direction and clarity in their lives.

Marked By Stature

If we want our kids to grow in wisdom, stature, and favor like Jesus, how should we pray when it comes to stature? *Merriam-Webster*'s definition of stature speaks both to physical height as well as status or reputation; both are key areas we can pray over our kids.

Praying for physical growth is praying that our kids remain healthy and develop into adults who can best accomplish God's plans for them. It's remembering that our bodies are God's temple, so we are called to care for them with the same concern and reverence we would show the physical church. It's praying over our kids' physical relationships, their decisions related to alcohol and drugs, their health, and praying over everything that impacts their bodies.

Along with physical growth, stature includes praying over our kids' reputations. Our reputation has the power to lead people to Christ or, if not done well, ruin our witness. It's what the world looks at to see if we practice what we preach. Knowing that we're called to live a life worthy of the gospel, let's pray that our kids grow a reputation consistent with their faith.

| 1 CORINTHIANS 6:19–20 | 1 CORINTHIANS 13:11 | PROVERBS 22:1 | PHILIPPIANS 1:27 |

I'm grateful for:

_____

_____

_____

_____

_____

_____

_____

I'm praying for:

_____

_____

_____

_____

_____

_____

_____

prayer:

Lord, we know you're more concerned with our heart than our physical appearance, so cultivate in [name] a heart that's marked by their faith in you. Guide each of my children to make decisions with both their body and reputation that honors you.

Marked By Favor

"FOR THE LORD GOD IS A SUN AND SHIELD; THE LORD BESTOWS FAVOR AND HONOR; NO GOOD THING DOES HE WITHHOLD FROM THOSE WHOSE WALK IS BLAMELESS."

PSALM 84:11

As we continue praying wisdom, stature, and favor for our kids, it's notable that Jesus was growing in all aspects of his life: mentally (in wisdom), physically (in stature), and spiritually (in favor with God). What a great reminder to pray over all the areas of our kids' lives, not limiting our requests to God.

It's abundantly clear we already have God's favor when we consider our name is written in the book of life despite our unworthiness. But as we pray God's continued favor over our children, we're simply asking him to accomplish things in their lives that would be impossible for them to do on their own.

David experienced God's favor in his face-off with Goliath, the Israelites saw God's favor when the Red Sea parted, and Sarah definitely had God's favor when she received word of her pregnancy.

The good news about God's favor is that he's looking for people to bless with it. We're told that "the eyes of the Lord search the whole earth in order to strengthen those whose hearts are fully committed to him" (2 Chronicles 16:9 NLT). In other words, God is literally looking across the earth for those he can bless because he loves us and wants to make our lives significant for his glory.

God's favor is unlimited and unmistakable in our lives, but we're best positioned to receive it when we're obedient, walking in step with him, and surrendering to his purposes.

Let's pray that our kids live lives God can bless, allowing his favor on all that they do.

GOD SPEAKS:

PSALM 90:17   EPHESIANS 2:8–9   NUMBERS 6:25–26   PROVERBS 3:1–2

I'm grateful for:

_____
_____
_____
_____
_____
_____
_____

I'm praying for:

_____
_____
_____
_____
_____
_____
_____

Lord, thank you for showing your great favor on us. You give us significance and purpose far beyond what we could do on our own. Empower [name] to live each day in a way that you can bless, teaching them daily the importance of obedience to your word.

Marked By Faith

"FEAR NOT, FOR I AM WITH YOU; BE NOT BE DISMAYED, FOR I AM YOUR GOD. I WILL STRENGTHEN YOU, I WILL HELP YOU; I WILL UPHOLD YOU WITH MY RIGHTEOUS RIGHT HAND."

ISAIAH 41:10 ESV

God is not surprised when we are fearful. In fact, the Bible is packed full of Scripture reminding us that we don't need to fear *anything* because God's love and protection are perfect.

When we choose to follow God, it's not signing up for the easy road. We will face challenging times over and over again, and the choice will be ours: Are we going to choose faith in God or surrender to fear in the face of uncertainty?

Let's help our kids pick faith over fear remembering these things:

- We're instructed to take our worries to God in prayer (1 Peter 5:7).
- We have assurance that he hears us when we pray (Psalm 34:17).
- God promises he will love and protect us no matter what we face (Deuteronomy 31:6).

In John 16:33, Jesus very plainly offers that in this world there will be trouble. But, in Christ, we need not fear, for he has overcome the world. In other words: let's remind our kids to be courageous, knowing that no matter what they face, Jesus has already beaten it!

JOSHUA 1:9   PSALM 34:4   2 TIMOTHY 1:7   PSALM 27:1

I'm grateful for:

_____

_____

_____

_____

_____

_____

I'm praying for:

_____

_____

_____

_____

_____

_____

prayer:

Lord, remind us that you are the author and creator over all things. You control the rising of the sun, the orbiting of the galaxies, and each and every star in the sky is placed there by you. Teach [name] to trust you in the difficulties each day. Replace fear with faith, knowing you have power over all things.

Marked By Identity

"BEFORE I FORMED YOU IN THE WOMB I KNEW YOU,
BEFORE YOU WERE BORN I SET YOU APART."

JEREMIAH 1:5

In a world saturated by social media, it can feel like an uphill battle raising kids who are confident in who Jesus says they are, not in who the world professes they are. Our culture critiques us based on looks, talents, failures, and accomplishments. Thankfully, the Bible gives the real story of our identity, reminding us that we are:

- Adopted as a sons and daughters of Christ (Romans 8:15)
- Chosen by God to declare his praise (1 Peter 2:9)
- Created with a purpose that God prepared in advance (Ephesians 2:10)
- Citizens of heaven (Philippians 3:20)
- Fully known and accepted by God (Psalm 139:1–4)

When our kids are marked by their true identity in Christ, they can live free from the exhausting cycle of trying to please others in order to gain approval. Only in the wake of this freedom can they chase after the person Jesus created them to be, not who our culture wants them to be.

Pray for our children to know that they are valuable, loved, seen, chosen, and good enough—not because of who they are, but because of whose they are.

GOD SPEAKS:

EPHESIANS 2:10 | JEREMIAH 31:3 | **JOHN 15:16** | **ROMANS 8:1**

I'm grateful for:

_____
_____
_____
_____
_____
_____
_____

I'm praying for:

_____
_____
_____
_____
_____
_____
_____

prayer:

Carefully, meticulously, intentionally—that's how you created every single one of your children. You made no mistakes in the creation process, and you knitted us together in the direct image of yourself. Lord, remind [name] that you alone assign value and that their value is secure and unchanging.

Marked By Contentment

"I AM NOT SAYING THIS BECAUSE I AM IN NEED,
FOR I HAVE LEARNED TO BE CONTENT WHATEVER
THE CIRCUMSTANCES."

PHILIPPIANS 4:11

At one point, John D. Rockefeller was the world's richest man and the first billionaire in America. When a reporter asked him how much money is enough, he responded, "Just a little bit more."

"A little bit more" is our culture's mantra. And it's not just limited to more money. We want more friends, more toys, more accolades, more popularity, more recognition, more respect, more security (and on and on and on).

At the end of the day, contentment isn't about our possessions, it's about our heart. So often we think we're discontent because of our job or bank account, but really our discontentment is a struggle with God's measure of provision for our lives.

In Philippians, Paul writes about being content whatever the circumstances. In doing so, he gives us a significant hint as to how contentment works: it's learned. It's consistently taking ourselves back to the cross, knowing that only through the lens of the gospel can we move from grumbling about what we don't have to gratitude for what we do have but don't deserve.

Let's pray that our kids can grasp the gift of contentment in a culture of "a little bit more," allowing them to fully appreciate God's provision in their own life while celebrating what he's doing in the lives of others.

GOD SPEAKS:

I'm grateful for:

_____

_____

_____

_____

_____

_____

I'm praying for:

_____

_____

_____

_____

_____

_____

prayer:

Lord, help my kids to live marked by contentment. Teach them to value people over possessions, appreciating that all their needs are already met in you. Reveal the greed, entitlement, and idolatry that leads to being discontent, and bring [name] back to a posture of gratitude no matter their circumstances.

Marked By Godly Relationships

"TWO ARE BETTER THAN ONE, BECAUSE THEY HAVE A GOOD
RETURN FOR THEIR LABOR: IF EITHER OF THEM FALLS DOWN,
ONE CAN HELP THE OTHER UP. BUT PITY ANYONE WHO FALLS
AND HAS NO ONE TO HELP THEM UP."

ECCLESIASTES 4:9–10

On her wedding anniversary—and just weeks after unexpectedly losing her young husband—a friend posted this short tribute: "We made a good team and completed each other. When I failed, he stepped in and where he failed, I stepped in. It was a partnership made in heaven and ordained by God."

This is a modern-day paraphrase of the Ecclesiastes verses describing godly relationships. It's spouses, friends, pastors, and mentors who pick us up when we fall down and build us up when we're struggling. It's those who see bigger potential in us than we can see for ourselves and pray God's biggest plans for us when we don't have the strength to pray for ourselves.

Godly relationships are easily identified because they bear such impact, love, and support that we somehow know the purpose is greater than just for our pleasure. Rather, it is God-ordained and for his glory.

As we pray for godly relationships for our children, pray that the Lord guards and anoints every relationship that impacts their lives. Pray for the Lord to bless them with deep, biblical friendships like Ruth and Naomi, godly mentors who speak truth like Nathan did to David, and spouses with an unrelenting love like Jacob and Rachel.

GOD SPEAKS:

PROVERBS 22:24–25   ECCLESIASTES 4:12   PROVERBS 27:17   PROVERBS 17:17

I'm grateful for:

_____

_____

_____

_____

_____

_____

I'm praying for:

_____

_____

_____

_____

_____

_____

prayer:

Lord, we were created to have relationships that draw us closer together and closer to you. Bless my children with friends, spouses, mentors, and others who build them up and point them back to you. Protect them from influences that are not your best in their lives. Teach [name] not just the importance of having godly friendships but also the gift of being a godly friend.

19

Marked By An Undivided Heart

"TEACH ME YOUR WAY, LORD, THAT I MAY RELY ON YOUR
FAITHFULNESS; GIVE ME AN UNDIVIDED HEART,
THAT I MAY FEAR YOUR NAME."

PSALM 86:11

We're called to teach our kids to love Jesus when they wake up, when they go to bed, on the way to baseball, on vacation, coming home from preschool, getting dressed for prom, when someone was mean to them, and everywhere in between. We're training them to live for Jesus in all circumstances.

As parents, it often means we're less concerned with academic potential and more interested in our child's heart for the lonely kid at lunch. It's relentlessly praying that our kids' inclinations to pursue popularity won't dilute the truth of their calling and identity in Christ. It's a mindset shift to the eternal when everyone around them seems focused on the temporal.

But, even with the best of intentions, our hearts become so easily divided this side of heaven. It happens when our commitment to Jesus starts to be overshadowed by our desire for comfort, convenience, entitlement, and entertainment.

As we pray this week for undivided hearts, we're praying that our kids understand at an early age the importance of an unwavering commitment to Jesus. It's praying that they have a God-given resolve to follow his word and his calling on their lives, whatever the cost.

I'm grateful for:

_____
_____
_____
_____
_____
_____

I'm praying for:

_____
_____
_____
_____
_____
_____

prayer:

Lord, teach us to appreciate that the small things of earth will someday be the big things in heaven. Teach [name] the significance of an undivided heart, marked by a commitment to following you—even when it's the harder path. Give our family a new spirit of determination to seek you and rely on your faithfulness.

Marked By God's Word

"DO NOT MERELY LISTEN TO THE WORD, AND SO DECEIVE YOURSELVES. DO WHAT IT SAYS."

JAMES 1:22

Many of us have heard Bible stories for as long as we can remember. We learned about a young boy named David defeating a huge giant with a slingshot, an honorable man named Noah building an ark having never experienced rain, and the story of Daniel walking unharmed out of a lions' den because of God's protection.

As children, these stories were entertaining. As adults, they are the foundations of truth by which we're called to live.

Being marked by God's word means we don't just hear it; we are changed by it. As parents, we commit to teaching our kids God's word when they are little so that the foundational truths of Scripture are planted in their souls for when they grow older.

We're praying for our kids to gain an understanding of the bigger picture of God's word this week, that they understand how God gets the greatest glory when we boldly face our giants in God's strength, like David did. We're praying that God will call them to obey when it makes no earthly sense, like Noah did. And, as they grow older and weather some long, hard places of suffering, they will know they were never alone, like Daniel did.

LUKE 11:28   HEBREWS 4:12   ISAIAH 40:8   MATTHEW 7:24

I'm grateful for:

_____

_____

_____

_____

_____

_____

I'm praying for:

_____

_____

_____

_____

_____

_____

prayer:

Lord, your word never returns empty. We claim this truth as we raise our kids in Scripture, praying that you give them a deeper understanding of the Bible and its priority for their lives. Keep [name] from simply hearing your word, but give it life and meaning that changes the way they live.

Marked By Generosity

"DO NOT STORE UP FOR YOURSELVES TREASURES ON EARTH,
WHERE MOTHS AND VERMIN DESTROY, AND WHERE THIEVES
BREAK IN AND STEAL. BUT STORE UP FOR YOURSELVES
TREASURES IN HEAVEN."

MATTHEW 6:19–20

Everything we have has been given to us by God.

When we really stop and think about this truth, it can't help but reframe how we operate in light of God's generosity toward us. The gospel calls us to be generous, not just because it benefits those around us, but because it benefits us.

To be marked by generosity, our kids need a few foundational truths:

- God owns it all, and we are simply stewards of his wealth on earth (1 Peter 4:10).
- Generosity is a matter of the heart, and giving is an act of worship (1 John 3:17).
- God's generosity is unmatched when you consider the gift of Jesus (Romans 5:8).

Generosity is not just a financial matter. Our kids can practice generosity even now by having a compassionate heart, a willingness to include others, advocating for the underdog, and freely extending forgiveness.

When we give to God, we never lose. Instead, we gain the opportunity to participate in his larger kingdom ministries. Being faithful in little leads to opportunities to be faithful in much (Luke 16:10).

I'm grateful for:

_____

_____

_____

_____

_____

_____

I'm praying for:

_____

_____

_____

_____

_____

_____

prayer:

Lord, if you didn't provide us with one more thing this side of heaven, we would still be overwhelmed by your generosity at the cross. Give [name] a heart of generosity, teaching them that our greatest gain comes from giving away what was never ours to begin with.

Marked By Thanksgiving

"GIVE THANKS TO THE LORD, FOR HE IS GOOD;
HIS LOVE ENDURES FOREVER."

PSALM 107:1

The Pilgrims celebrated the first Thanksgiving in 1621 despite having recently lost half of their population to a harsh winter filled with contagious diseases. By celebrating their first successful harvest, they reminded a young nation of the importance of giving thanks in all circumstances.

Today, most of us spend Thanksgiving day knee-deep in the traditions of turkey, football, and family time; however, as Christians, we also celebrate on a deeper level, knowing that all of our gratitude is owed to the Lord.

We're praying this week that our kids live marked by thankfulness—even in the hard places. When the road they face is difficult, pray that they give thanks that Jesus goes before them and has won every battle waged against them. We're promised that God will work everything according to his purposes, so we can be assured that God desires to bring out the good in whatever they are facing.

Paul reminds us from his jail cell in Rome that, in Jesus, we can sing, make music, and be thankful in all things (Ephesians 5:19–20).

Ingratitude is a sin, thankfulness is a choice, turkey is dry.

Happy Thanksgiving!

| PSALM 100:4 | COLOSSIANS 3:17 | PSALM 107:8–9 | 1 THESSALONIANS 5:16–18 |

I'm grateful for:

_____

_____

_____

_____

_____

_____

_____

I'm praying for:

_____

_____

_____

_____

_____

_____

_____

prayer:

Lord, every good and perfect gift comes only from you, and we have the privilege of celebrating that this week. As we celebrate Thanksgiving as a family, give my kids a deep connection with you as the giver of all good things in their lives. Help [name] to be marked by thanksgiving no matter their circumstances.

Marked By Light

"THE LIGHT SHINES IN THE DARKNESS, AND THE
DARKNESS HAS NOT OVERCOME IT."

JOHN 1:5

A quick glance at the news confirms that our culture's moral code is growing further away from the truths of Scripture. With the widening of this gap, our kids will likely face more scrutiny and persecution for living biblically than many of the generations before them.

Even so, we have the message of truth and are called to share it. In the middle of a world of darkness and uncertainty, our culture desperately needs to hear the gospel message that Jesus loved us to the point of death so that we might live forever (John 3:16).

Each new day presents opportunities for our children to shine God's light in the darkness around them. It's accomplished by refusing to conform to the world. Instead, pray that your children live set apart in how they talk, what they prioritize, and how they do life. Living counterculturally provides the opportunity to point others to the true source of our light: Jesus.

Ask the Lord to ground our kids in the confidence and determination necessary to stand firm in a culture that rejects absolute truth. Pray that they won't pass up a single chance to shine the light of Jesus in a dark world.

I'm grateful for:

_____

_____

_____

_____

_____

_____

_____

I'm praying for:

_____

_____

_____

_____

_____

_____

_____

prayer:

Jesus, you alone change lives. Help [name] to be brave enough to live set apart for you. As our culture grows further away from the truths of the gospel, give us more opportunities to share our faith in you with love and conviction.

Marked By Integrity

"THE GODLY WALK WITH INTEGRITY; BLESSED ARE
THEIR CHILDREN WHO FOLLOW THEM."

PROVERBS 20:7 NLT

When we think about God's character, we probably think of attributes like righteousness, holiness, mercy, love, and justice. The Bible reminds us that the character of God is unchanging: he's the same yesterday, today, and forever (Hebrews 13:8). He's dependable, he's consistent, he's compassionate, and he's a God of integrity who desires the same for us.

Integrity is more than how we respond in a given situation or a prescribed moral code we follow when life gets tricky. The word integrity comes from the Latin root integer, meaning whole. It's a reference to our whole person, both who we are in public and in private.

D. L. Moody has said that character is what you are in the dark. The same could be said of integrity.

As we pray integrity over our kids this week, we're asking the Lord to guide them to live with biblical standards in all areas of their lives. At one point or another, integrity will impact their finances, profession, marriage, parenting, calling, and even the words that come out of their mouths. Let's pray that "what they are in the dark" reflects God's light in all areas of their lives.

1 PETER 3:16 | PROVERBS 12:22 | **2 CORINTHIANS 8:2** | PROVERBS 21:3

I'm grateful for:

_____

_____

_____

_____

_____

_____

I'm praying for:

_____

_____

_____

_____

_____

_____

prayer:

Lord, you call us to a higher standard because you love us, you're for us, and you know what's best for us. I ask you to give [name] the desire to live with integrity in all areas of their life. Guide us as a family to value honesty and live set apart.

Marked By Joy

"BUT THE ANGEL SAID TO THEM, 'DO NOT BE AFRAID. I BRING YOU GOOD NEWS THAT WILL CAUSE GREAT JOY FOR ALL THE PEOPLE.'"

LUKE 2:10

The odds are pretty good that you will sing "Joy to the World" at a Christmas service this season. It's a classic Christmas carol with a great reminder of why we have joy.

> Joy to the world, the Lord is come!
> Let earth receive her King!

These simple words explain the reason for our joy as Christians: Jesus has come. But how do we live with joy in a world with such real suffering?

Max Lucado talks about two different types of joy: contingent joy and courageous joy. Contingent joy is based on our circumstances and how things are going in life. Courageous joy is based in Jesus and is with us no matter what we're facing.

Contingent joy focuses on the situational; courageous joy focuses on the eternal.

Joni Eareckson Tada is an author, speaker, and artist who was paralyzed as a teenager as a result of a diving accident. She says her joy comes from knowing that "God permits what he hates to accomplish what he loves." She's focused on the eternal.

Joy is one of the attributes the world sees in us and doesn't understand; it's a great testimony, especially when it's displayed in the hard places of life. Let's pray for our kids to be marked by joy, not just at Christmas but at all times, because it's not based on today but eternity.

Joy to the world, the Lord has come!

| PHILIPPIANS 4:4 | PSALM 118:24 | 1 THESSALONIANS 5:16–18 | ROMANS 12:12 |

I'm grateful for:

_____

_____

_____

_____

_____

_____

_____

I'm praying for:

_____

_____

_____

_____

_____

_____

_____

prayer:

Jesus, you are the reason we have joy. In complete humility, you came to earth as a baby, to pay the price for our sins so that we might live eternally. Reveal in [name] a joy that's rooted not in their circumstances but in you alone.

Marked By The Nativity

"'THE VIRGIN WILL CONCEIVE AND GIVE BIRTH TO A SON,
AND THEY WILL CALL HIM IMMANUEL'
(WHICH MEANS 'GOD WITH US')."

MATTHEW 1:23

When I was growing up, my family had a beautiful Christmas nativity in our living room that had been hand-painted by my grandmother. I remember the meticulously adorned kings, the elegant white angel, and the pristine animals more fit for a banquet than a barn.

It would have met anyone's definition of the perfect nativity set except for one thing: we lost baby Jesus.

This was quite the conundrum since it wasn't something a quick trip to Hobby Lobby could remedy. But, even without Jesus, my mom continued to display her nativity because the significance behind my grandmother's handmade gift meant more than the splendor of a perfect nativity set.

Christmas is full of pretty decorations, sparkly lights, and all the things that make this time of year special. But, much like my mom's choice to continue displaying our nativity set, we're praying that our kids grasp the significance behind the splendor as we celebrate Jesus' birth.

The significance comes in praying for a faith like Mary, who was willing to say yes even when it didn't make sense. Or learning to walk in obedience like Joseph, who did the God-ordained things, not just the easy ones. It's going any distance to meet Jesus like the wise men did. It's approaching him like the lowly shepherds, in complete awe and wonder of the newborn King.

Pray this week that our kids don't just see Christmas for all of its splendor but live marked by the significance of Jesus' birth and the message of the nativity.

| LUKE 2 | ISAIAH 9:6 | JOHN 1:14 | LUKE 2:14 |

I'm grateful for:

_____

_____

_____

_____

_____

_____

_____

I'm praying for:

_____

_____

_____

_____

_____

_____

_____

prayer:

Lord, allow the significance of the nativity to mark our kids as we celebrate your birth. Give [name] the faith of Mary, the obedience of Joseph, and the awe and reverence of the shepherds. Strip away the splendor of a secularized Christmas, showing our family the deep love you showed by coming to earth as a baby.

Marked By Numbering Days

"TEACH US TO NUMBER OUR DAYS, THAT WE MAY
GAIN A HEART OF WISDOM."

PSALM 90:12

Every seasoned parent knows how quickly time passes when you're in the throes of raising kids. It seems like one day they're toddlers and the next day you're visiting colleges. Despite being cautioned that "the days are long, but the years are short," it's still hard to appreciate how fast it passes until you're on the other side looking back.

As we start a new year, it's a great time for our families to remember to number our days because time is fleeting. Counting our days is not meant to be mathematical, but missional. It's living today as if you have no tomorrow. It's making the most of every God-given opportunity, knowing that missed opportunities are often our greatest regrets.

David understood the brevity of life when he wrote, "You have made my days a mere handbreadth; the span of my years is as nothing before you. Everyone is but a breath, even those who seem secure" (Psalm 39:5).

As we pray for our kids to number their days, ask the Lord to give them the wisdom to evaluate every decision and opportunity through the lens of eternity.

PSALM 39:4   EPHESIANS 5:15   JAMES 4:14–15   PSALM 144:4

I'm grateful for:

_____

_____

_____

_____

_____

_____

_____

I'm praying for:

_____

_____

_____

_____

_____

_____

_____

prayer:

Lord, you are the God of the past, present, and future. We claim your promise that for every good work you begin in our kids, you will carry it to the point of completion. Please impress upon [name] the importance of numbering their days, knowing there is nothing more important or significant than the plans you have for them in this moment.

Marked By Protection

"THE LORD WILL KEEP YOU FROM ALL HARM—HE WILL WATCH
OVER YOUR LIFE; THE LORD WILL WATCH OVER YOUR COMING
AND GOING BOTH NOW AND FOREVERMORE."

PSALM 121:7–8

It's hard to feel safe when the news all around us tells a different story. But we can trust in the Lord's protection because there is nothing he cannot do. He created everyone and everything in the universe and has complete control over every detail of it.

As parents, it's often especially difficult to trust God's protection when it comes to our kids. We constantly need reminding that our best defense on their behalf is a commitment to praying for them. Even when we question God's protection over them, we can trust that he's sovereign, good, and never acts contrary to his loving nature.

The real truth is that nothing can ultimately harm those who rest in the grip of our heavenly Father. Paul reminds us of this truth when he says: "Neither death nor life, nor angels nor demons, neither the present nor the future, nor any powers, neither height nor depth, nor anything else in all creation, will be able to separate us from the love of God that is in Christ Jesus our Lord" (Romans 8:38–39).

Pray that when the world seems really scary to our kids, they will remember the One who created the world. He's our fortress and protector, guiding our very steps and guarding our every path.

GOD SPEAKS:

ISAIAH 54:17 | PSALM 34:7–9 | 2 THESSALONIANS 3:3 | DEUTERONOMY 31:6

I'm grateful for:

_____

_____

_____

_____

_____

_____

_____

I'm praying for:

_____

_____

_____

_____

_____

_____

_____

prayer:

Lord, we pray for protection over our children that only comes from you. We pray not just for their physical protection but also for their spiritual health and protection. Please remind [name] that faith in you brings healing for all eternity because nothing can separate us from you. Keep them in your presence and protect them both today and always.

Marked By Truth

"SANCTIFY THEM BY THE TRUTH; YOUR WORD IS TRUTH."

JOHN 17:17

During one of our recent *Pardon the Mess* podcast interviews with Sadie Robertson, I ran across some great parenting advice as she shared what had helped her through the struggles of her teenage years. She said that anytime she went to her mom for advice, her mom would always "meet her with Jesus."

Meeting our kids with Jesus just might be the most significant thing we can do in our kids' lives. Satan is the father of lies, looking for ways to misguide and deceive us at every turn. Only in Jesus will we find real truth, especially in a culture that rejects absolute truth.

As we pray that our kids are marked by truth, we have the opportunity to point them to the truth in Scripture no matter what they are facing. Kids marked by truth will not waver with every opinion thrown their way. Kids marked by truth will live with a higher standard, even when it's unpopular. Kids marked by truth will hear the lies of the Enemy and recognize them as just that: lies.

Cissie Graham Lynch, daughter of Franklin Graham, said it this way in an Instagram post: "Whatever lies Satan tells you in life or whatever chains he has on you, you tell him Jesus holds victory! Although, the world faces darkness, Jesus is the LIGHT of the world."

I'm grateful for:

_____
_____
_____
_____
_____
_____

I'm praying for:

_____
_____
_____
_____
_____
_____

prayer:

Jesus, you are the truth that overcomes the lies of the Enemy and shines light in the darkness. Help my family to identify the lies we're believing, replacing them with the truth of your word. Give [name] an increasing understanding of who you are and your great love for them. Fill our families with hope, joy, and truth that comes only from you.

Marked By Compassion

"BE KIND AND COMPASSIONATE TO ONE ANOTHER, FORGIVING EACH OTHER, JUST AS IN CHRIST GOD FORGAVE YOU."

EPHESIANS 4:32

Compassion is one of the defining characteristics of God. He's sympathetic to our struggles and burdened by what burdens us. But, even more than simply feeling compassion and sympathy toward us emotionally, his compassionate nature moves him to act on our behalf.

This compassion turned to action is most evident when we consider the cross. "While we were still sinners, Christ died for us" (Romans 5:8). That's the overwhelming grace behind a compassionate God working all things for the good of his children.

If compassion is central to the gospel, what should it look like in our lives? Henri Nouwen describes it this way: "Compassion asks us to go where it hurts, to enter into the places of pain, to share in brokenness, fear, confusion, and anguish. Compassion challenges us to cry out with those in misery, to mourn with those who are lonely, to weep with those in tears. Compassion requires us to be weak with the weak, vulnerable with the vulnerable, and powerless with the powerless."

As we pray compassion for our kids this week, we're praying that it's more than a fleeting emotion. Rather, we're praying that it's evident in their actions. Pray that they stand up for the vulnerable, fight for the oppressed, and are intolerant of injustices around them.

| 1 PETER 3:8 | 2 CORINTHIANS 1:3–4 | COLOSSIANS 3:12 | LAMENTATIONS 3:22–23 |

I'm grateful for:

_____

_____

_____

_____

_____

_____

I'm praying for:

_____

_____

_____

_____

_____

_____

prayer:

Lord, your word calls us to have compassion and love for others. Please give [name] a compassionate heart to see the things that burden you and a spirit of determination to help others in whatever way you lead. Slow us down and give us discernment to see the needs around us and not to tolerate the things that break your heart.

Marked By Hope

"BUT THOSE WHO HOPE IN THE LORD WILL RENEW THEIR STRENGTH. THEY WILL SOAR ON WINGS LIKE EAGLES; THEY WILL RUN AND NOT GROW WEARY, THEY WILL WALK AND NOT BE FAINT."

ISAIAH 40:31

A few years ago, Pew Research released a poll revealing that seven in ten US teens considered anxiety and depression a major problem among their peers. Of those participating in the poll, 61 percent indicated they felt pressure to get good grades, while 29 percent felt pressure to look good and 28 percent felt pressure to fit in socially.

Considering that our culture's expectations are so often arbitrary and impossible to meet, it's not surprising that our kids struggle with anxiety and depression. When the world ties our worth to materiality and performance, it feels hopeless because we're only as good as our most recent accomplishment or latest accolade.

But, as Christians, our hope is in the Lord. Practically speaking, that means we're not looking to the world to meet our greatest needs and desires, Rather, we look to God. Biblical hope is not just desiring for something good to happen in our lives; it's a confident expectation that God will actually do it.

There are so many reasons for our kids to be hopeful in the Lord:

- He has good plans for their lives (Jeremiah 29:11).
- He leads and teaches them in his ways (Psalm 32:8).
- He will fulfill his greater purpose in their lives (Psalm 138:8).
- He will establish their plans (Proverbs 16:3).
- He promises to work all things together for their good (Romans 8:28).

The Pew Research statistics confirm what we already know: we need to diligently pray that our kids are not weighed down by impossible standards of our culture, but that they will be marked by a hope found only in the Lord.

GOD SPEAKS:

EPHESIANS 1:18 | JEREMIAH 29:11 | MARK 9:23 | PSALM 33:18

I'm grateful for:

_____
_____
_____
_____
_____
_____

I'm praying for:

_____
_____
_____
_____
_____
_____

prayer:

Lord, there is no hope without you. Use [name] as an instrument to take your hope to those around them. Take our days, Lord—the good, the bad, the easy, the hard—and show us the greater picture of hope found only in you.

Marked By Confidence

"BUT BLESSED IS THE ONE WHO TRUSTS IN THE LORD,
WHOSE CONFIDENCE IS IN HIM."

JEREMIAH 17:7

We all want to raise confident kids, but the hard part is making sure their confidence comes from the right source: God himself. We live in a culture that esteems strong finances, good looks, prestigious jobs, and realized dreams—none of which are lasting or fulfilling.

When we look to find our confidence in the things of this world, we will never find satisfaction. Solomon, among the wisest and wealthiest of all time, describes the pursuits of this world as "utterly meaningless" (Ecclesiastes 1:2). He pursued everything the world had to offer only to conclude that there's "nothing new under the sun" so we should only "fear god and keep his commandments."

The great irony of the gospel is that only in acknowledging our insufficiency can God do his greatest work by strengthening us.

Let's pray that our kids are marked by confidence in things with lasting value:

- The promise that God will complete every good work in them (Philippians 1:6)
- Their identity as children of God (2 Corinthians 5:17)
- The good news of the gospel and their eternity with Jesus (John 3:16)
- The opportunity to approach God boldly in prayer, knowing that he hears them (Hebrews 4:16)

| PSALM 27: 3 | PHILIPPIANS 4:13 | PSALM 139:13–14 | ROMANS 8:28 |

I'm grateful for:

_____

_____

_____

_____

_____

_____

I'm praying for:

_____

_____

_____

_____

_____

_____

_____

Lord, this world is filled with uncertainty that threatens to rock our confidence. But you are steadfast and reliable, showing favor on your children and building them up to accomplish your purposes. Please give [name] a confident spirit marked by their reliance on you.

Marked By Purity

"HOW CAN A YOUNG PERSON STAY ON THE PATH OF PURITY?
BY LIVING ACCORDING TO YOUR WORD."

PSALM 119:9

The idea of raising pure kids in an impure culture can feel like an impossibly tall order as parents. Defining purity can be confusing and is oftentimes limited to discussions of physical relationships or online accountability. We sometimes mistakenly make purity a goal our kids must achieve, staying away from certain things or even keeping on a prescribed path until the finish line of marriage.

But purity is not an accomplishment; it's a relationship, as Noel Bouche of Pure Hope Ministries said on our *Pardon the Mess* podcast. It's a relationship with Jesus, who comes to redeem us from the sin of this world and purify us to himself (Titus 2:14). He renews our minds and equips us to overcome our earthly temptations. He cleanses us and makes us new creations. He gives hope that is everlasting and brings healing when we fall short.

Biblical purity is bigger than a checklist of things our kids should or should not do, but instead focuses on the bigger picture of the lifelong pursuit of Jesus. It's not about our ability to perform but about Jesus' transforming power within us.

There's nothing wrong with praying for our kids to have purity in their physical relationships, the way they dress, the motivation behind their actions, their pursuit of Jesus, and the music and media that fill their minds. But let's also pray that if and when they fall short, they know that the Lord stands ready to forgive them and give them a new beginning.

COLOSSIANS 3:5   1 TIMOTHY 4:12   MATTHEW 5:8   TITUS 2:13–14

I'm grateful for:

_____

_____

_____

_____

_____

_____

I'm praying for:

_____

_____

_____

_____

_____

_____

prayer

Lord, please bring [name] to you, purifying them through a renewing of their heart and mind. Give my kids the freedom to come to me no matter what they have seen or done, knowing that, as a family, we will offer grace and seek your wisdom. Help my kids to take captive their thoughts and find companionship with those seeking a pure heart and a life of righteousness.

Marked By God's Presence

"AND SURELY I AM WITH YOU ALWAYS,
TO THE VERY END OF THE AGE."

MATTHEW 28:20

Despite being the most connected generation in history, today's kids feel increasingly isolated and lonely. Recent studies show that social media actually adds to feelings of loneliness, especially when it's used as a substitute for real connection.

As Christians, we may also feel periods of social isolation, but with Jesus there's no spiritual isolation because we're never alone.

The presence of God is a core message of the Bible. God was with Adam and Eve in the garden in Genesis, and the truth of God's presence continues all the way to Revelation, where we're promised an eternity with God (in a new heaven and new earth).

Living in God's presence is significant for our kids because it's the assurance they are never overlooked, unseen, or insignificant. He is always near to them, making it impossible to be separated from his love and provision. It's a great confidence boost knowing that the God of the universe is next to them as a friend, father, protector, and provider.

We can find joy in all circumstances because, no matter what we're facing, we do it in the presence of Jesus. David says it this way: "In your presence there is fullness of joy; at your right hand are pleasures forevermore" (Psalm 16:11 ESV).

ROMANS 8:38–39 | JOSHUA 1:9 | PSALM 23:4 | DEUTERONOMY 31:8

I'm grateful for:

_____

_____

_____

_____

_____

_____

_____

I'm praying for:

_____

_____

_____

_____

_____

_____

_____

prayer.

Lord, help our kids to understand that you are with them at this very moment. Whether they are studying, eating, playing, or even worrying about their future—remind them that you are completely and fully present in their lives. Take away any loneliness that [name] may face, reminding them they are significant, loved, and seen.

Marked By Self-Discipline

"FOR THE MOMENT ALL DISCIPLINE SEEMS PAINFUL RATHER THAN PLEASANT, BUT LATER IT YIELDS THE PEACEFUL FRUIT OF RIGHTEOUSNESS TO THOSE WHO HAVE BEEN TRAINED BY IT."

HEBREWS 12:11 ESV

Nobody lacks self-discipline like our precious two-year-olds. Their language repertoire is heavy with words like *no, mine,* and *more*—typically accompanied with a hearty side of theatrics. As cute as it might be when they are young (or not), a lack of self-discipline creates some big issues later in life.

Self-discipline (or lack thereof) will impact every part of our kids' lives, including their dating relationships, finances, online accountability, marriage, physical health, and even their occupations. The author of Hebrews reminds us that discipline isn't fun in the moment, but it's a key step in the pathway to righteousness.

The good news is that self-discipline isn't just a matter of mustering up enough willpower. Rather, it's a God-given perspective that the greater reward in waiting is better than the immediate temptation we're facing. Warren Wiersbe says it this way: "Discipline means giving up the good and the better for the best. There is nothing wrong with food or fun, but if they interfere with your highest goals, then they are hindrances and not helps."

Let's ask God to give our kids the self-discipline to look away, walk away, or find a way to pass on anything that interferes with God's highest goals in their lives. Jesus is worth waiting for, and self-discipline eliminates the pain and discouragement of settling for less than his best in their lives.

| 1 CORINTHIANS 9:24 | PROVERBS 25:28 | 2 TIMOTHY 1:7 | 1 CORINTHIANS 9:27 |

I'm grateful for:

_____
_____
_____
_____
_____
_____
_____

I'm praying for:

_____
_____
_____
_____
_____
_____
_____

prayer:

Lord, help [name] to have the self-discipline to pass up the good in order to accomplish the great you have planned for them. Give my children an eye for your bigger picture in all areas of their lives, knowing the ultimate goal of righteousness is worth waiting for.

Marked By God's Certainty

"WE CAN MAKE OUR PLANS, BUT THE LORD
DETERMINES OUR STEPS."

PROVERBS 16:9 NLT

We just don't know what we don't know.

History gives us some pretty funny stories of people who tried to predict the future but got it embarrassingly wrong. One great example is from 1962, when a record executive told the Beatles they "have no future in show business" because four-piece groups with guitars are a thing of the past.

Oops.

The only thing we can be certain about this side of heaven is that our lives are going to be uncertain. We had no idea that a global pandemic would shut down the United States in 2020, and we don't know what's headed our way in 2025.

But God does.

In the middle of uncertainty for Joshua, God reminded him that "every place that the sole of your foot will tread upon I have given to you" (Joshua 1:3 ESV). The message to Joshua is the same message for us: with God directing our steps, not even one of them is unexpected or without purpose to the One who authors them all.

This week, we're praying for our kids to understand that what's uncertain to them is anything but unexpected or unplanned to God. Knowing that, we can put our trust in the One who not only knows the future but also writes it.

ROMANS 8:28   PHILIPPIANS 1:6   ISAIAH 45:2   PROVERBS 3:6

I'm grateful for:

_____

_____

_____

_____

_____

_____

_____

I'm praying for:

_____

_____

_____

_____

_____

_____

_____

prayer:

Lord, you don't just know what the future holds, you are the future. Help [name] to stand firm in the face of uncertainty, knowing that you determine their steps and, in doing so, go before and behind them with power and authority over all things. We don't know what we don't know—but you do.

Marked By Surrender

"THEN JESUS SAID TO HIS DISCIPLES, 'WHOEVER WANTS TO BE MY DISCIPLE MUST DENY THEMSELVES AND TAKE UP THEIR CROSS AND FOLLOW ME. FOR WHOEVER WANTS TO SAVE THEIR LIFE WILL LOSE IT, BUT WHOEVER LOSES THEIR LIFE FOR ME WILL FIND IT.'"

MATTHEW 16:24–25

"I Surrender All" is a classic hymn that gained notoriety when Rev. Billy Graham began using it as the invitation song during his revivals. The words have such a great message for walking with Jesus:

> All to Jesus I surrender, all to him I freely give;
> I will ever love and trust him, in his presence daily live.
> I surrender all, I surrender all,
> All to thee, my blessed Savior, I surrender all.

Surrender is the antithesis of trying to "work" our way into a right relationship with God. A surrendered life allows the Spirit of God to enter into us, shaping us into something greater than we could be on our own.

The first and most significant act of surrender we can pray over our kids' is their choice to surrender to the lordship of Christ by accepting Jesus as their savior. But, even after our kids have accepted Christ, we can pray that they surrender their words, plans, dreams, finances, and relationships to the Lord.

Pray for our kids to have the discipline to surrender all they are to the Lord each day, committing to live in a way that's pleasing and brings him glory.

| PHILIPPIANS 2:13 | JAMES 4:7 | JOHN 3:30 | PSALM 32:8 |

I'm grateful for:

_____

_____

_____

_____

_____

_____

I'm praying for:

_____

_____

_____

_____

_____

_____

prayer:

Lord, you become more when we become less. Please guide [name] to accept you as their Savior and surrender their lives to your glory. Help them know that surrendering to you is a lifelong process as they trust you with their burdens, fears, dreams, and aspirations.

Marked By Refinement

"IN ALL THIS YOU GREATLY REJOICE, THOUGH NOW FOR A LITTLE WHILE YOU MAY HAVE HAD TO SUFFER GRIEF IN ALL KINDS OF TRIALS. THESE HAVE COME SO THAT THE PROVEN GENUINENESS OF YOUR FAITH—OF GREATER WORTH THAN GOLD, WHICH PERISHES EVEN THOUGH REFINED BY FIRE—MAY RESULT IN PRAISE, GLORY AND HONOR WHEN JESUS CHRIST IS REVEALED."

1 PETER 1:6–7

The final stage in gold production is refinement, the process of using heat to remove impurities from metal. After the gold is refined, only the most valuable qualities remain because the impurities and lesser qualities have been eliminated.

Scripture says that God is refining us. Even though we're created in his exact image, we are free-willed human beings riddled with sin and impurities that don't line up with who we were created to be. Just as the refinement of gold takes place in the heat of fire, refinement in our own lives often happens in the "furnace of affliction" (Isaiah 48:10).

As parents, we want to keep our kids from the hard places, so we find ourselves stepping in when they face difficulties. But what if God is working most significantly in the hard places in their lives? What if changing their circumstances prevents God from changing their heart?

As we're praying for our kids to be marked by refinement, let's not ask God to remove their obstacles but rather to remove their impurities. Let's pray that when the heat intensifies, our kids learn to trust that the One who allows the fire will also bring them through it.

I'm grateful for:

_____

_____

_____

_____

_____

I'm praying for:

_____

_____

_____

_____

_____

Lord, you refine us so that we are cleansed from unrighteousness and become a purer version of who you created us to be. We ask you to take all of the difficulties and trials that [name] will face and use them as an opportunity to see a clearer picture of you. Thank you for loving us too much to leave us as we are. Refine us for your glory.

Marked By Armor

"PUT ON THE FULL ARMOR OF GOD, SO THAT YOU CAN TAKE YOUR STAND AGAINST THE DEVIL'S SCHEMES. FOR OUR STRUGGLE IS NOT AGAINST FLESH AND BLOOD, BUT AGAINST THE RULERS, AGAINST THE AUTHORITIES, AGAINST THE POWERS OF THIS DARK WORLD AND AGAINST THE SPIRITUAL FORCES OF EVIL IN THE HEAVENLY REALMS."

EPHESIANS 6:11–12

Most of us don't spend a lot of time contemplating how to fight against the devil's schemes, but Scripture does. Thankfully, Jesus has already won our ultimate battle by his death on the cross and resurrection from the grave. But, even then, there will still be trouble in this world because we have a real Enemy who seeks to steal, kill, and destroy (John 10:10).

As we face the visible (and often invisible) battles each day, Satan's success hinges on catching us unprepared and with our guard down. Let's pray that our kids are battle-ready by wearing the armor of God, as seen in Ephesians 6:13–17:

- The belt of truth: Pray that God's truth will defeat the enemy's lies in their lives.
- The breastplate of righteousness: Pray that they withstand attacks of impurity and wrongdoing by clinging to righteousness.
- Feet fitted with the gospel of peace: Pray for a willingness to go and share the gospel.
- The shield of faith: Pray for protection from doubt, fear, and anxiety.
- The helmet of salvation: Pray for a mind controlled by God.
- The sword of the Spirit: Pray that God's word is their offense, knowing it's sharper than any sword.

EPHESIANS 6:13–17	1 THESSALONIANS 5:6	1 PETER 5:8	1 CORINTHIANS 16:13

I'm grateful for:

_____

_____

_____

_____

_____

_____

I'm praying for:

_____

_____

_____

_____

_____

Lord, the battles waged against our kids will be difficult and often unseen. Help them to be ready for anything they face through your protection and power. Mark [name] with a readiness that only comes from you. Prepare them with every tool necessary for victory in your name.

Marked By Fruit

"BUT THE FRUIT OF THE SPIRIT IS LOVE, JOY, PEACE,
FORBEARANCE, KINDNESS, GOODNESS, FAITHFULNESS,
GENTLENESS AND SELF-CONTROL."

GALATIANS 5:22–23

As we celebrate Easter, we have the opportunity to pray that the power of the cross impacts every area of our kids' lives. It is an incredible assurance knowing that, by accepting Jesus, our kids have a new eternal destination. But we're also praying for a daily life transformation.

When our kids become Christians, we should begin looking for (and hopefully seeing) fruit in their lives. Jesus said those who follow him will produce spiritual fruit, and it's by this fruit you will know them (Matthew 7:20).

In Galatians, Paul describes some attributes of a life without Christ, including anger, idolatry, jealousy, selfishness, impurity, and strife. In contrast, with Christ we start to see the spiritual fruit of love, joy, peace, patience, kindness, gentleness, and self-control. Thankfully, this is not simply a checklist of things we're constantly trying to achieve. Instead, it's produced by allowing the Holy Spirit to work within us.

Without even trying, our kids will produce fruit that's visible to the world around them. This fruit can either be produced by the Holy Spirit or produced by their own spirit. Our prayer is that our kids will submit to the Holy Spirit's leadership, resulting in less of their own fruit and more of his.

This week, let's pray that Easter Sunday impacts the way our kids live on Monday and that they produce fruit that leads others to trust Jesus and his great sacrifice at the cross.

He is risen! He is risen indeed!

MATTHEW 7:17–18 · ROMANS 8:6 · EPHESIANS 4:1–3 · ROMANS 15:13

I'm grateful for:

_____

_____

_____

_____

_____

_____

I'm praying for:

_____

_____

_____

_____

_____

prayer:

Lord, thank you for your sacrifice at the cross. Allow our gratitude for the significance of Easter to impact how we live every day. Grow our kids in obedience and holiness, naturally leading them to produce spiritual fruit. Help [name] to submit to your Holy Spirit in both the small and big ways, making their life a clearer reflection of you.

"LOVE THE LORD YOUR GOD WITH ALL YOUR HEART
AND WITH ALL YOUR SOUL AND WITH ALL YOUR
MIND AND WITH ALL YOUR STRENGTH."

MARK 12:30

Remember the lawyer who tried to trick Jesus by asking him to name the greatest commandment? (Lawyers, am I right?)

Jesus, knowing this guy's antics, responded with, "Love God with all of your heart, soul, mind, and strength." If we break it down, what does it look like to love God with all of our heart?

Our heart is not just critical to our health; it's also the epicenter of our spiritual life. It's central to our thoughts and actions, where we spend money, and even the words that come out of our mouths. When Jesus talks about loving God with all our heart, he's referencing our emotions and decisions.

In order for us to love God with all of our hearts, we have to prioritize spending time with him and in his word. When we spend time with God, we start wanting to do the things that are pleasing to God and we care about the things that he cares about. Having time with our creator enables us to know what he wants for our lives, and we can't help but pursue him and the things he values and wants for our families.

Let's pray this week that our kids learn to love God with all of their hearts, beginning with prioritizing time with him and pursuing him in all that they do.

I'm grateful for:

_____
_____
_____
_____
_____
_____
_____

I'm praying for:

_____
_____
_____
_____
_____
_____
_____
_____

prayer:

Lord, teach us to show our love for you, not just with our words, but with our lifestyle. Lead [name] to prioritize time in your word and learn to pursue you in all that they do. Remind us that loving you means also loving our neighbor. Make us aware of the needs we can meet around us.

Marked By Our Soul

"WHAT GOOD IS IT FOR SOMEONE TO GAIN THE WHOLE WORLD, YET FORFEIT THEIR SOUL?"

MARK 8:36

Loving God with all of our soul sounds very important, but what exactly is our soul?

Our soul lies deep down inside of us and is our very core. It's the invisible part of us that connects us with God. It is where we are most at home, and it's the most fundamental driver of who we are from the inside out. If you strip away all of our outward actions and how we choose to portray ourselves (or how others may define us), the soul is our truest self.

To love the Lord with all of our soul, we've got to be faithful in private. We've got to be devoted to the things that drench our soul in Jesus and be willing to drop the things that don't. It's spending time in prayer confessing what's in our soul, not just in our mind.

As we pray for our kids to love God with all of their souls this week, let's pray that they learn to love him with the very core of who they are—not by what they intellectually believe about him, or how they serve him, or what they communicate to others by their faith, but truly learning to love Jesus from the core of their being.

Pray for the Lord to reveal the depths of their soul and teach them how to love him with all that they are.

| PSALM 119:81 | PSALM 63:8 | DEUTERONOMY 4:29 | MATTHEW 10:28 |

I'm grateful for:

_____

_____

_____

_____

_____

_____

I'm praying for:

_____

_____

_____

_____

_____

Lord, we confess to spending a disproportionate amount of time worrying about our earthly bodies, usually at the expense of our soul. Please teach [name] how to love you from their very core, giving priority to the only part of us that will live eternally.

Marked By Our Mind

"WE DEMOLISH ARGUMENTS AND EVERY PRETENSION THAT SETS ITSELF UP AGAINST THE KNOWLEDGE OF GOD, AND WE TAKE CAPTIVE EVERY THOUGHT TO MAKE IT OBEDIENT TO CHRIST."

2 CORINTHIANS 10:5

As we pray for our kids to love God with all of their minds, we have to consider that our mind is made up of our thoughts. So, in order to love God with all of our minds, we have to think about what fills our minds and how it impacts the way we love God.

Our thoughts are significant because they have the potential to grow our love for God or distract and pull us away from a relationship with him and his great plans for our life. The Enemy loves to get a hold of our thoughts and make us question God's goodness and protection in our life.

For our kids to love God with all of their minds, we're praying that they "take captive" all the thoughts that are destructive, not instructive. This process of taking captive their thoughts is accomplished by knowing God's word so that their thoughts are weighed against the truth of Scripture.

It also comes by considering what's going into their minds and how that's fueling (or lessening) their love for God. It's praying that they evaluate the movies they watch, the music they listen to, and the voices they allow to speak into their lives.

Since our kids' thoughts have the greatest impact on loving God with all of their minds, let's take time to pray over their thoughts and ask God to help them take each one captive.

I'm grateful for:

_____

_____

_____

_____

_____

_____

_____

I'm praying for:

_____

_____

_____

_____

_____

_____

_____

prayer:

Lord, teach us to love you in all of the different areas of our life, including our minds. If our minds are made up of our thoughts, teach us to take captive our thoughts and bring them in line with your truth. Be with [name], helping them to guard what they allow into their mind so that it always honors you.

Marked By Our Strength

"EACH OF YOU SHOULD USE WHATEVER GIFT YOU HAVE
RECEIVED TO SERVE OTHERS, AS FAITHFUL STEWARDS OF
GOD'S GRACE IN ITS VARIOUS FORMS."

1 PETER 4:10

As we wrap up the greatest commandment, we're focused on how to love God with all of our strength. Contrary to how it sounds, loving God with all of our strength is not a reference to our physical strength. The Hebrew word used for strength in the context of the greatest commandment is *me'od,* which is translated as "much" or "very."

Loving God with all of our strength is loving God with our "much-ness." It's using our possessions, our time, our talents, our parenting, our volunteering—everything we've got—to love God and live for him. Said differently, wherever the Lord has planted you and with whatever resources he's provided, use all your strength to love him smack-dab in the middle of it all.

As we pray for our kids to love God with all of their strength, we're praying that they use all of their party-planning skills, math aptitude, athleticism, and social media acumen for God's greatest glory. It's taking the seemingly small places in their life and asking the Lord to use it in every possible way for his bigger purposes.

Spend time this week asking the Lord to use your kids' gifts to bring God glory. Pray that he uses them for his greater purposes right where he has them, teaching them to love the Lord with all of their much-ness and strength.

I'm grateful for:

_____

_____

_____

_____

_____

_____

_____

I'm praying for:

_____

_____

_____

_____

_____

_____

_____

_____

prayer:

Lord, thank you for all the gifts and talents you've given our family. I pray that you will guide my children to use these gifts generously for your glory. With all of the much-ness you've given [name], remind them to serve those around them as they learn to love you with all of their strength.

Marked By By Endurance

"DO YOU NOT KNOW THAT IN A RACE ALL THE RUNNERS RUN, BUT ONLY ONE GETS THE PRIZE? RUN IN SUCH A WAY AS TO GET THE PRIZE."

1 CORINTHIANS 9:24

The Christian life is more like a marathon than a sprint, requiring significant endurance if we're going to make it through the obstacles we face along the way. From the day we accept Christ until we see him face-to-face, we're continually building up endurance so we can best run the race set out for us.

Having endurance in the context of our faith means we're always in training mode, getting ready for the hard places of discouragement and suffering that will challenge our readiness for the race. We build up our endurance practically by staying true to the basics: things like spending daily time with God, finding Christian community, memorizing Scripture, and seeking discipleship.

This week, we're praying for our kids to run their spiritual races with endurance. We're praying that they keep their eyes on Jesus, setting aside anything that weighs them down or keeps them from running effectively. In a culture falling further away from biblical standards, our kids will need endurance and tenacity to live God's way and not the world's.

Let's challenge our kids to run well so they will hear Jesus say at the finish line, "Well done, my good and faithful servant" (Matthew 25:23).

PHILIPPIANS 3:14   ROMANS 5:3–4   2 TIMOTHY 4:7   HEBREWS 10:36

I'm grateful for:

_____

_____

_____

_____

_____

_____

_____

I'm praying for:

_____

_____

_____

_____

_____

_____

_____

prayer:

Lord, before you created even one of us, you set us apart for your purposes. Give [name] the endurance to run the race you have planned for their life. Help them to stay the course when they run up against obstacles along the way, reminding them of the importance of putting in the daily work so they are prepared for anything they face.

Marked By Humility

"DO NOTHING OUT OF SELFISH AMBITION OR VAIN CONCEIT. RATHER, IN HUMILITY VALUE OTHERS ABOVE YOURSELVES, NOT LOOKING TO YOUR OWN INTERESTS BUT EACH OF YOU TO THE INTERESTS OF THE OTHERS."

PHILIPPIANS 2:3–4

We're raising kids in a culture that basks in recognition and praise, making it difficult to strike the balance of teaching our kids to be confident in their God-given identity while also exuding a humble spirit. Humility is not ignoring their giftings, but it's teaching them to be willing to use them in a way that draws attention to the Giver of the gift rather than the gift itself. Humility is also not a call to raise silent or passive kids. Rather, it's teaching them a quiet and meek spirit before God.

Jesus is the perfect model of humility. He came to earth in the form of a baby and lived a blameless life so he could die on the cross and give us new life. He more than deserved recognition and acknowledgment for his heavenly status, yet he chose to demonstrate humility because of his commitment to the Father's will and the larger gospel story. He was righteously indignant when necessary but gentle and loving in leading his flock.

We're praying this week for our kids to humbly serve others, admitting their mistakes, and recognizing that all praise and glory belongs to the Lord as the giver of all good gifts (James 1:17). Let's also ask the Lord to guide them in being passionate and outspoken when appropriate, but also disciplined enough to be quick to listen, slow to speak, and slow to anger (James 1:19).

| EPHESIANS 4:2 | ROMANS 12:16 | JAMES 4:10 | COLOSSIANS 3:12 |

I'm grateful for:

_____

_____

_____

_____

_____

_____

_____

I'm praying for:

_____

_____

_____

_____

_____

_____

_____

prayer:

Lord, you're the perfect model of living humbly while making a kingdom impact on those around you. Give [name] a spirit of humility and the desire to bring you glory, even when it comes with no acknowledgment. Help them to honor others above themselves and to live in your confidence so they don't need praise or acceptance from others.

Marked By Remembering

"THEN SAMUEL TOOK A STONE AND SET IT UP BETWEEN MIZPAH AND SHEN. HE NAMED IT EBENEZER, SAYING, 'THUS FAR THE LORD HAS HELPED US.'"

1 SAMUEL 7:12

The Israelites were in desperate need of a victory against the Philistines. Just as they were convincing themselves it was a lost cause, Samuel cried out to God and received an answer in the form of deafening thunder that scared away the enemy and secured an Israelite victory.

Orthodox battle move? No. God protecting his people? Absolutely.

No sooner than they finished their victory lap, Samuel stopped everyone in their tracks to make a critical point. He grabbed a stone as a memorial and named it Ebenezer, translated as "the Lord has helped us to this point."

Samuel knew their battle win was significant from a tactical perspective, but he also knew the more significant win was the reminder that God had protected them in the past and he'd just done it again.

Our kids need the same reminder today that Samuel gave way back then: The God who has taken care of us up to this point will do it again. He is faithful and trustworthy.

What are the Ebenezers in your family? Where do you need to start laying down stones as reminders to your family that God's faithfulness in the past shows he's trustworthy for the future?

DEUTERONOMY 7:9	2 THESSALONIANS 3:3	LAMENTATIONS 3:22–23	PSALM 86:15

I'm grateful for:

_____

_____

_____

_____

_____

_____

I'm praying for:

_____

_____

_____

_____

_____

_____

_____

Lord, remind us to always pass down the stories of your faithfulness. Mark [name] with a good memory of your provision, giving them confidence to trust your heart when they can't see your hand. Help us to celebrate the places where you've given us victory, making a lasting memorial of your faithfulness for generations to come.

Marked By Mission

"THEREFORE GO AND MAKE DISCIPLES OF ALL NATIONS,
BAPTIZING THEM IN THE NAME OF THE FATHER AND OF THE SON
AND OF THE HOLY SPIRIT, AND TEACHING THEM TO OBEY EVERYTHING
I HAVE COMMANDED YOU. AND SURELY I AM WITH YOU ALWAYS,
TO THE VERY END OF THE AGE."

MATTHEW 28:19–20

We've spent this school year praying for our kids to be marked by the things of God. We've prayed that they live with integrity, confidence, generosity, endurance, and much more. But these are nothing more than admirable qualities if they aren't used for God's kingdom purposes.

Before Jesus ascended to heaven, he gave us our mission. He told us to go and make disciples, sharing the story of his grace and love.

The Great Commission is our central mission. The same is true for our kids.

We're God's Plan A for spreading the gospel. There's no backup plan, there's no contingency, and there's nobody else to tag in for our spot.

But it all starts at home. It happens in the seemingly insignificant moments of reading Bible stories to our toddlers and the really hard places of pointing them to Jesus on the heels of their biggest mistakes and greatest obstacles.

Please let us never underestimate the significance of our jobs as moms and dads, discipling our kids to share the gospel to the next generation.

Let's wrap up this school year by praying that our kids will be marked by the mission of Jesus, doing it with truth, discipline, purity, and every other characteristic of God we've prayed over them this year.

1 PETER 2:9   MARK 16:15   1 PETER 3:15   ECCLESIASTES 12:13–14

I'm grateful for:

_____

_____

_____

_____

_____

_____

_____

I'm praying for:

_____

_____

_____

_____

_____

_____

_____

prayer:

Lord, thank you for the gift of my children and the privilege of praying over them this school year. Please mark their lives with a determination to fulfill the mission you created for them before they were ever born. Give [name] the wisdom to pursue you every day and a spirit of urgency in following your plans for their life.

Before we say goodbye...

As we end the school year, I'm once again reminded of how quickly time passes. Yesterday, we were buying new school shoes. Today, we're applying sunscreen while questioning if we signed the kids up for enough summer camps.

My hope is that this prayer journal has provided you with opportunities to slow down for a few minutes each week to reflect on God's goodness and pray for his provision over your kids. We know that God hears us when we pray (1 Peter 3:12), so let's give thanks that he's working for our good even in the places where we can't yet see it.

Let me encourage you to take time to go back and share some of your prayer entries with your children, showing them God's faithfulness in their lives when we present our requests to him.

Have a wonderful summer!

Cynthia Yanof

CYNTHIA YANOF
PARDON THE MESS

We want to be better parents. We want to give our children the love and attention they need. But our lives are so busy, and we're stretched so thin, it can be hard to do more than the status quo.

So we created Christian Parenting to give parents everywhere the practical and spiritual help they need, on as many platforms as possible, for free.

With the right resources given to you in the right ways, growth can happen in the midst of the busyness. You don't need to be perfect. In fact, growth comes as you embrace becoming perfectly imperfect.

Go to ChristianParenting.org to find out how.

ABOUT PARDON THE MESS

Cynthia Yanof hosts the *Pardon the Mess* podcast, which belongs to the Christian Parenting podcast network.

On the podcast you'll hear great words from guests like Priscilla Shirer, Bob Goff, Christine Caine, and many others!

Alongside the podcast, *Pardon the Mess* offers resources like prayer journals, identity cards, devotionals, and many other ways for parents to connect with the Lord.

Listen to *Pardon the Mess* podcast on iTunes or wherever you access your podcasts, and check out the other *Pardon the Mess* resources on pardonthemess.org.

ABOUT CYNTHIA YANOF

Cynthia Yanof is a wife to Mike and a mom to Kate (17), Brett (13), and JB (4). She loves Jesus, her family, foster care, and having lots of friends around her at all times.

She uses her quick wit and sense of humor to talk about the ups and downs of parenting in a way that's pleasing to the Lord, but also with a firm commitment to not taking herself too seriously.

16   **John D. Rockefeller** "John D. Rockefeller," New World Encyclopedia Online, accessed June 4, 2020, http://newworldencyclopedia.org/entry/John_D._Rockefeller.

30   **D. L. Moody has said** D. L. Moody, The Quiet Hour (Illustrated), (Independently published, 2019).

32   **two different types of joy** Max Lucado, "Contagious Joy," last modified February 2016, https://maxlucado.com/contagious-joy/.

40   **"Whatever lies Satan tells you"** Cissie Graham Lynch (@cissiegrahamlynch), Instagram photo, April 12, 2020, https://www.instagram.com/p/B-4rRQcFulp/

42   **Henri Nouwen describes it** Henri Nouwen, "Compassion," accessed June 3, 2020, https://henrinouwen.org/meditation/compassion/.

44   **Pew Research released a poll** A.W. Geiger and Leslie Davis, "A growing number of American teenagers – particularly girls – are facing depression," Pew Research, last modified July 12, 2019, https://www.pewresearch.org/fact-tank/2019/07/12/a-growing-number-of-american-teenagers-particularly-girls-are-facing-depression/.

50   **social media actually adds to feelings of loneliness** Sherry Amatenstein, "Not So Social Media: How Social Media Increases Loneliness," Psycom, last modified November 16, 2019, https://www.psycom.net/how-social-media-increases-loneliness/.

52   **Warren Wiersbe says it** Warren Wiersbe, The Wiersbe Bible Commentary: New Testament (Colorado Springs, CO: David C. Cook, 2007), 481.

54   **the Beatles . . . "have no future"** Josh Sanburn, "Top 10 Failed Predictions: Four-Piece Groups with Guitars Are Finished," Time, October 21, 2011, http://content.time.com/time/specials/packages/article/0,28804,2097462_2097456_2097466,00.html.